A Day in the LIFE OF...

A POLICE OFFICER

Written by Noah Leatherland

Enslow
PUBLISHING

Published in 2025 by Enslow Publishing, LLC
2544 Clinton Street
Buffalo, NY 14224

© 2024 BookLife Publishing Ltd.

Written by:
Noah Leatherland

Edited by:
Rebecca Phillips-Bartlett

Designed by:
Amelia Harris

Cataloging-in-Publication Data

Names: Leatherland, Noah, 1999-.
Title: A police officer / Noah Leatherland.
Description: Buffalo, NY : Enslow Publishing,
    2025. | Series: A day in the life of… | Includes
    glossary and index.
Identifiers: ISBN 9781978541894 (pbk.) |
    ISBN 9781978541900 (library bound) |
    ISBN 9781978541917 (ebook)
Subjects: LCSH: Police--Juvenile literature.
Classification: LCC HV7922.L43 2025 |
    DDC363.2--dc23

Manufactured in the United States of America

CPSIA compliance information: Batch #CW25ENS:
For further information contact Enslow Publishing LLC
at 1-800-398-2504.

Please visit our website, www.enslowpublishing.com.
For a free color catalog of all our high-quality books,
call toll free 1-800-398-2504 or fax 1-877-980-4454.

Find us on 🅕 🅸

Image Credits

All images are courtesy of Shutterstock.com, unless otherwise specified. With thanks to Getty Images, Thinkstock Photo and iStockphoto. Recurring – Lee Charlie, TWINS DESIGN STUDIO, RoseRodionova, Drazen Zigic, PeopleImages.com - Yuri A, IGORdeyka. Cover – PeopleImages.com - Yuri A, Anatolir. 2–3 – Alexander Oganezov. 4–5 – Drazen Zigic, Tyler Olson. 6–7 – Keith Homan. 8–9 – ZikG. 10–11 – MariVolkoff. 12–13 – Giannis Papanikos. 14–15 – PeopleImages.com - Yuri A. 16–17 – PeopleImages.com - Yuri A. 18–19 – Yurii Kiliian, Abscent Vector. 20–21 – Alexander Oganezov, Aspects and Angles, Wise ant. 22–23 – PeopleImages.com - Yuri A.

CONTENTS

Words that look like this can be found in the glossary on page 24.

A DAY IN THE LIFE

Grown-ups do all kinds of jobs. Each job has its own tasks and challenges. They all need different skills. Do you know what job you want to do when you are older?

Chef

Librarian

A police officer is someone who helps others in their community. Their job is to stop crimes, protect people from danger, and help them when they are in trouble.

OFFICER

POLICE

STARTING THE DAY

POLICE DEPARTMENT

POLICE

POLICE

Police officers start their day by arriving at the police station. They find out what tasks they have been given for the day and make a plan for how they will tackle them.

However, anything can happen in a police officer's day. The police are called whenever there is an emergency. Police officers might have to stop what they are doing to go and help someone.

CHECKING EQUIPMENT

Police officers use a lot of special equipment every day. They need to make sure it is working properly before they go out in the community.

Vest

Radio

Handcuffs

A police officer's equipment helps them stay safe.

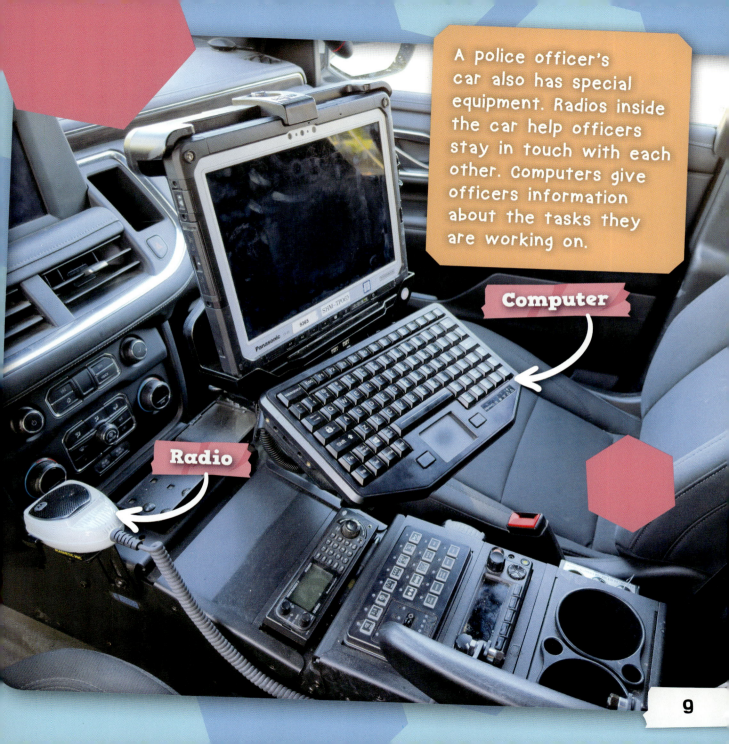

A police officer's car also has special equipment. Radios inside the car help officers stay in touch with each other. Computers give officers information about the tasks they are working on.

Computer

Radio

PATROLLING THE AREA

Sometimes, police officers are given the task of patrolling an area. This means that they keep watch over the area. They are ready in case anyone needs their help.

On patrol, police officers might look for anything suspicious. They keep an eye out for anything that might become a problem. They also watch traffic and make sure everyone is driving safely.

Police officers might stop someone's car to make sure they are driving carefully.

EMERGENCY!

If there is an emergency, police officers on patrol might get a call on their radio asking for their help. They jump in their police car and rush over to where they are needed.

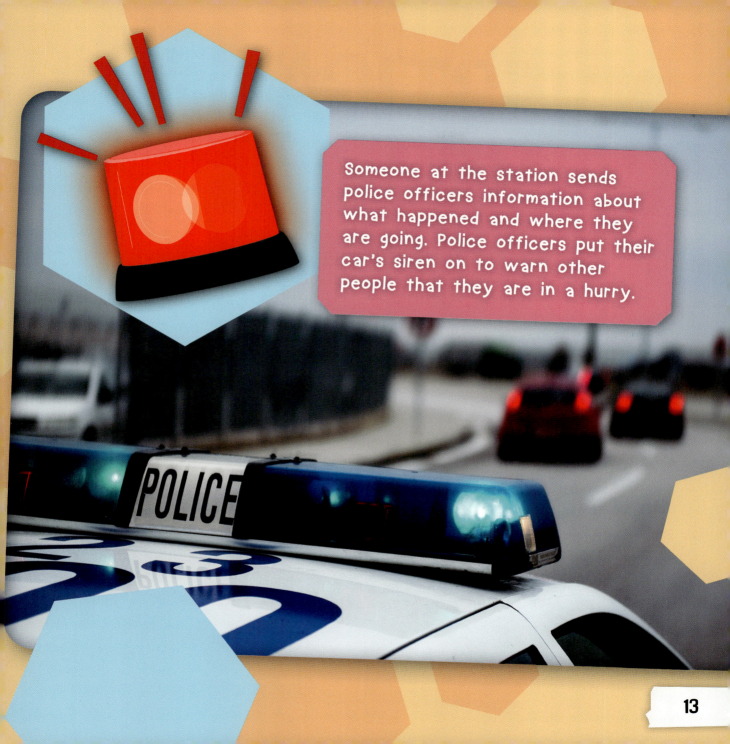

Someone at the station sends police officers information about what happened and where they are going. Police officers put their car's siren on to warn other people that they are in a hurry.

Investigating Crimes

Some of the emergencies police officers are called to are when a crime has happened. Once they have checked that everyone is OK, officers need to find out what happened.

Police officers are trained to help people who are very upset.

CRIME SCENE DO NOT ENTER

Police officers talk to the people who might have seen or heard what happened. The officers ask questions and take statements. They look around to see if they can find any evidence.

LOOKING AT EVIDENCE

Once the police officers have collected as much evidence as they can, they look through it closely. They see if they can find any clues from what they found or what people said.

Some pieces of evidence might not be ready right away. A forensics team might look closer at some evidence in a laboratory. This can give the police officers more clues to solve the crime.

DOING PAPERWORK

Whenever a police officer deals with an incident, they write a report about it. They write down everything that happened and all the actions they took.

Police officers need good literacy skills to write their reports.

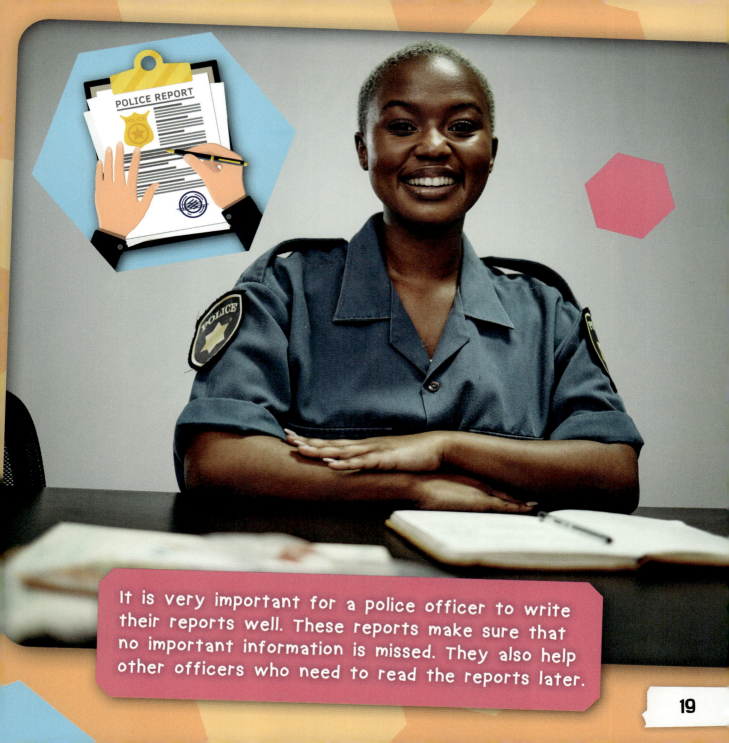

It is very important for a police officer to write their reports well. These reports make sure that no important information is missed. They also help other officers who need to read the reports later.

IN THE COMMUNITY

Police officers help with many other things in the community. When there is a big gathering, such as a parade or a sports event, police will be around to make sure everyone stays safe.

Police officers might also visit schools to teach children how to stay safe. Officers make sure they are seen around the community. That way, people know they can come to them for help.

WOULD YOU LIKE TO BE A POLICE OFFICER?

A police officer's day can involve a lot of different tasks. They might rush around town between emergencies or spend a day helping with an event. They need to be ready for anything.

Police officers need to make sure they communicate well. This includes how they speak with the community and how they write their reports.

Would you like to be a police officer?

OFFICER

POLICE

23

GLOSSARY

COMMUNICATE	to pass information between two or more things
COMMUNITY	a group of people who live and work in the same place
CRIMES	actions that are against the law
EVIDENCE	something that gives proof and can be used to give reason to believe in something
FORENSICS	science related to actions that are against the law
INCIDENT	an event where something has happened
LABORATORY	a place where scientists carry out experiments and research
LITERACY	the ability to read and write
STATEMENTS	accounts of something by people who saw it happen
SUSPICIOUS	not trustworthy

INDEX